Adding Alligators

and
Other Easy-to-Read Math Stories

by Betsy Franco

SCHOLASTIC
PROFESSIONAL BOOKS

New York • Toronto • London • Auckland • Sydney
Mexico City • New Delhi • Hong Kong • Buenos Aires

For Diane McCoy,
my expert on first-graders

Cover design by Josué Castilleja

Cover illustration by Liisa Chauncy Guida

Interior illustrations by Jane Dippold

Interior design by Sydney Wright

ISBN: 0-439-24984-8
Copyright © 2001 by Betsy Franco
All rights reserved. Printed in the U.S.A.

Contents

Introduction

In today's busy classroom, connecting math and literacy is both fun and practical. *Adding Alligators and Other Easy-to-Read Math Stories* provides 26 short, engaging stories along with companion word problems that help children build important math and reading skills at the same time. Designed for emergent readers, these stories relate to math topics and include a variety of genres and formats. Children will enjoy simple poems and mini-books, a nursery rhyme, a folktale, a read-aloud play, and much more. The lively stories and appealing illustrations motivate children to read the stories and solve the math problems.

Math Topics

These math stories and word problems are a great way to introduce young learners to problem-solving strategies while building key math skills. The following topics are covered in this book:

- Sorting
- Counting
- Comparing
- Skip-Counting
- Even and Odd Numbers
- Patterns
- Ordinal Numbers
- Addition
- Sums of 10
- Doubles
- Subtraction
- Groups of 10
- Graphing
- Measuring
- Ordering
- Money
- Time
- Calendar
- Shapes/Geometric Solids
- Symmetry
- Basic Fractions
- Pre-Multiplication
- Pre-Division

Problem-Solving Strategies

The word problems in this book can be used as a springboard for exploring a variety of basic problem-solving strategies. Here are some suggested strategies to share with your students.

Draw a Picture

Drawing a picture is a useful problem-solving strategy, especially for visual learners. Whenever appropriate, encourage children to draw pictures to help them visualize a problem. Many of the problems in this book include pictures that students can use in the problem-solving process.

Use Objects

Working with objects is a helpful strategy for primary learners. For example, in Going on a Field Trip, students use paper cars and paper children to find out how many cars are needed to fit various groups of children.

Guess and Check

Guessing and checking helps children determine the correct answer. For example, in Nina's Birthday, each animal brings 10 gifts. The frog brings 3 flies and some beetles. By testing different numbers in the equation 3 + ___ = 10,

children can guess and check to find how many beetles the fly brought.

Choose the Operation

Choosing the operation is an important basic strategy for successful problem solving. In Papa Bear Makes Dinner, children discover that subtraction is the best operation for determining how many carrots, potatoes, and other ingredients Papa has left to put in the soup. The problems are all phrased a little differently so that children can choose the operation each time.

Look for a Pattern

Recognizing patterns is an important mathematical skill. This book includes several stories in which children study the illustrations or text to find patterns. For example, in The Animal Parade, children first determine the pattern of animals marching in the parade and then continue the pattern.

Act It Out

Acting out a problem is especially helpful to kinesthetic learners. In Going on a Field Trip! children determine how many children will ride in each car. Acting this out can make the problem real for children. The read-aloud play, The Farm's Asleep, is also made to be acted out!

Use Logical Reasoning

Logical-mathematical thinkers will enjoy using logic to solve problems. In Frogs on a Log, children color the frogs according to a set of logical instructions, such as "The fourth frog has bumps on its back."

How to Use This Book

The math stories and problems in this book can be used in a variety of ways to meet your students' needs and interests. First, make a copy of the story and word problems for each student. Some stories are presented in the form of a mini-book. Show children how to assemble the mini-books by cutting out the boxes, arranging them in numerical order, and stapling them together along the left side.

You may wish to have children read the stories and solve the problems individually, in pairs, in small groups, or as a whole class. After children have solved the problems, review both the problem-solving strategies that can be used and the answers. (Answers are provided on pages 61–63.)

Here are some suggested ideas for using the activities:

- ◆ Display the story on an overhead projector, pocket chart, or chart paper. Then, read the story aloud together.

- ◆ Have each child store the stories and word problems in a Math Stories folder.

- ◆ Invite children to color the illustrations on the reproducibles.

- ◆ Have children read the stories and solve the problems with older student buddies.

- ◆ Encourage children to act out the stories after reading them.

- ◆ Create a bulletin board showing the problem-solving strategies children used to solve the problems.

- ◆ Have children collaborate to make up their own simple stories and companion math problems.

Name _____ Date _____

Sorting Circus Hats

The wind blew hard at the circus one day, and everyone's hat flew away.

Clown hats, top hats, big and small. The seals used their noses to sort them all!

Name _____ Date _____

Sorting Circus Hats

Cut out the hats on page 8.
Then follow the directions below.

Sort the hats by type.

(1) How many top hats are there? _____

(2) How many baseball caps are there? _____

Sort the hats by size.

(3) How many hats are big? _____

(4) How many hats are small? _____

Sort the hats by color.

(5) How many hats are gray? _____

(6) How many hats are white? _____

Adding Alligators and Other Easy-to-Read Math Stories Scholastic Professional Books

Name _____ Date _____

 # The Farm's Asleep: A Play

Characters

4 cows, 6 sheep, 2 horses, 7 pigs, 1 rooster, 1 narrator

Narrator: The sun went down.
The farm is asleep.
None of the animals make a peep.

Cows: Count the cows fast asleep.

Sheep: Count the sheep fast asleep.

Horses: Count the horses fast asleep.

Pigs: Count the pigs fast asleep.

Narrator: The sun comes up.
The day is new.

Rooster: Cock-a-doodle-doo!

Narrator: The rooster's up and the animals, too!

Sheep: Baaaa!

Pigs: Oink!

Horses: Naaaay!

Cows: Moooooooooo!

Adding Alligators and Other Easy-to-Read Math Stories Scholastic Professional Books

Name _____ Date _____

The Farm's Asleep: A Play

Answer the questions about the story.

1 How many cows were sleeping? _____

2 How many sheep were sleeping? _____

3 How many horses were sleeping? _____

4 How many pigs were sleeping? _____

5 Are there more pigs or cows? _____
Fill in > or < in the blank below:
7 pigs _____ 4 cows

6 Are there more horses or sheep? _____
Fill in > or < in the blank below:
2 horses _____ 6 sheep

7 Are there more pigs or sheep? _____
Fill in > or < in the blank below:
7 pigs _____ 6 sheep

Name _____ Date _____

The Baseball Team

The animals were bored one day.
They needed a brand-new game to play.
Frog said, "Baseball would be fun!
Let's make two teams with everyone!"

Some animals fly,
some hop, some run.
Now here's how long it takes each one:

Bird flew to first base in 2 seconds.
Frog hopped to first base in 5 seconds.
Cat ran to first base in 3 seconds.
Worm slithered to first base in 10 seconds.

Adding Alligators and Other Easy-to-Read Math Stories Scholastic Professional Books

Name _____ Date _____

The Baseball Team

Answer the questions about the story.
Use the hints to help you.

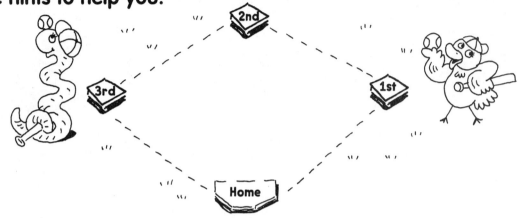

1 How long will it take Bird to fly around all the bases?

_____

Hint: It took Bird 2 seconds to fly to first base. Skip-count by 2s.

2 How long will it take Frog to hop around all the bases?

_____

Hint: It took Frog 5 seconds to hop to first base. Skip-count by 5s.

3 How long will it take Cat to run around all the bases?

_____

Hint: It took Cat 3 seconds to run to first base. Skip-count by 3s.

4 How long will it take Worm to slither around all the bases?

_____

Hint: It took Worm 10 seconds to slither to first base. Skip-count by 10s.

Pairs of Penguins

Penguins like to dive in pairs,
swim in pairs, and slide in pairs.

Sometimes there are 3 of them,
and then they can't all be in pairs.

But they don't really seem to care.
They slide together here and there!

Name _____ Date _____

Pairs of Penguins

Cut out the boxes below.
Then answer the questions.

(1) Try to group 6 penguins in pairs.
Can you group all of them? _____ Is 6 even or odd? _____

(2) Try to group 5 penguins in pairs.
Can you group all of them? _____ Is 5 even or odd? _____

(3) Try to group 7 penguins in pairs.
Can you group all of them? _____ Is 7 even or odd? _____

(4) Try to group 8 penguins in pairs.
Can you group all of them? _____ Is 8 even or odd? _____

Name _____ Date _____

The Animal Parade

The dogs and cats made friends one day.
They had a dog and cat parade.
Cat, dog, cat, dog, cat, dog, cat—
the animals lined up like that.

Then when the toads came by to play,
they lined up in a different way.
Cat, dog, toad, cat, dog, toad—
they marched in order down the road.

Adding Alligators and Other Easy-to-Read Math Stories   Scholastic Professional Books

Name _____

Date _____

The Animal Parade

Cut out the boxes on page 16.

Glue the boxes in the blanks to continue the patterns.

1

2

3

4 Now make up your own pattern with cats, dogs, and toads!

Patterns
All Around

The snake has stripes.

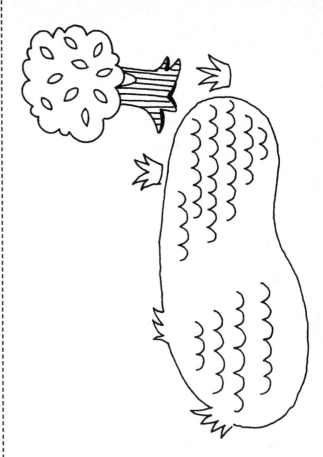

The waves make a pattern, too.

The bug has spots.

The bracelet has a pattern of white and blue.

Do you see patterns all around you? Draw a pattern here.

The shirt has a pattern of stripes and dots.

Now look at you and your classroom.

Name _____ Date _____

Patterns All Around

Follow the directions for each question.

(1) Continue the pattern
on the snake.

(2) Continue the pattern
on the bug.

(3) Continue the pattern
on the boy's shirt.

(4) Continue the pattern
on the bracelet.

Name _____ Date _____

Frogs on a Log

Read the poem.
Color the frogs to match the poem.
Then answer the questions about the poem.

Five little frogs are sitting on a log.
The first frog has 2 yellow spots.
The second one has 3 big brown dots.
The third frog's skin is red and black.
The fourth frog has some bumps on its back.
The fifth one is a dark green frog.
They all croak happily on the log!

1 Which frog has bumps on its back?

The _____ frog has bumps on its back.

Hint: Use an ordinal number word (<u>first</u>, <u>second</u>, <u>third</u>, and so on).

2 Which frog has brown dots? The _____ frog has brown dots.

3 What color is the fifth frog? The fifth frog is _____.

4 Another frog hopped on the log. It was the _____ frog to sit on the log.

Name _____ Date _____

Adding Alligators

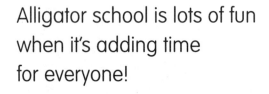

Alligator school is lots of fun
when it's adding time
for everyone!

Annie piles 3 blocks up tall.
She adds 4 more.
How many in all?

Alex puts 3 nuts in a cup,
puts 5 more in,
and gobbles them up.

Amy puts 2 bears on a mat,
then adds 6 more.
How many is that?

Alligators add things every day
in lots of fun
and yummy ways!

Adding Alligators and Other Easy-to-Read Math Stories Scholastic Professional Books

Name _____ Date _____

Adding Alligators

Answer the questions about the story.

1 How many blocks did
Annie use in all?

_____

2 How many nuts did
Alex eat in all?

_____

3 How many bears are
on Amy's mat in all?

_____

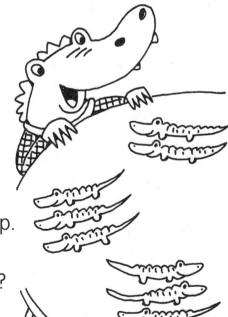

BONUS

Adam has lots of counting alligators.
There are 2 alligators in the first group.
There are 3 alligators in the second group.
There are 4 alligators in the third group.
How many alligators does he have in all?

_____

Name _____ Date _____

Pet Store

The crabs all grab.
The birds all cheep.
The hamsters play at hide-and-seek.
The mice all scurry.
The rabbits hurry.
The little pup is brown and furry.
But the only critter that I would take
is long and spotted—
it's Jake the Snake!

Count the animals in the picture.
Then write a number sentence for each problem.
The first one has been done for you.

(1) How many mice and hamsters are there in all? <u>6 + 3 = 9</u>   <u>9 animals</u>

(2) How many crabs and snakes are there in all? _____ _____

(3) Tim bought the mice and birds.
How many animals did Tim buy in all? _____ _____

(4) Beth bought the snakes and hamsters.
How many animals did Beth buy in all? _____ _____

(5) If the store gets 4 more crabs, how many crabs will it have in all?

_____ _____

Adding Alligators and Other Easy-to-Read Math Stories Scholastic Professional Books

The Three Wishes

Once upon a time, a fisherman helped a magic frog.

He showed the pole to his wife.

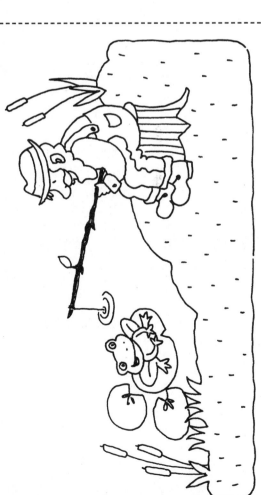

The frog said, "You may have 3 wishes." The fisherman wished for a new fishing pole.

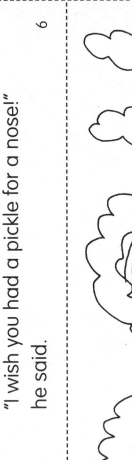

The fisherman got angry.
"I wish you had a pickle for a nose!" he said.

6

"I wish I had 3 more wishes," said the fisherman.
"This time, I would think before I wished."

8

His wife was upset.
"What a foolish wish!" she said.

5

"Help! Use your last wish to fix my nose!" said the wife.
And the fisherman did.

7

Name _____ Date _____

The Three Wishes

Write a number sentence to show each answer.

1 The fisherman got 3 wishes.
If he got 3 more wishes,
how many wishes would he have in all?

_____

2 A princess was given 4 wishes.
A prince was given 4 wishes.
How many wishes did they have in all?

_____

3 Suppose you were given 5 wishes.
Then suppose you were given 5 more wishes.
How many wishes would you have in all?

_____

BONUS

If you were given 3 wishes,
what would you wish for?

_____

_____

_____

Nina's Birthday

Squirrel brought 2 acorns and some walnuts.

Frog brought 3 flies and some beetles.

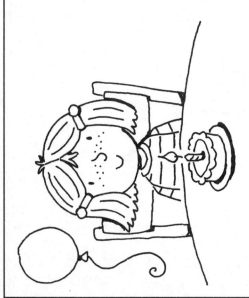

Nina invited her animal friends to her birthday party. Each animal brought 10 gifts.

Nina said, "Thank you. Thank you! It's the thought that counts!"

Bird brought 5 small worms and some big worms.

Dog brought 4 big bones and some small bones.

Name _____ Date _____

Nina's Birthday

Answer the questions about the story.
The first one has been done for you.

(1) How many beetles did the frog bring?

3 flies + ___7___ beetles = 10 bugs

(2) How many walnuts did the squirrel bring?

2 acorns + _____ walnuts = 10 nuts

(3) How many small bones did the dog bring?

4 big bones + _____ small bones = 10 bones

(4) How many big worms did the bird bring?

5 small worms + _____ big worms = 10 worms

Name _____ Date _____

Papa Bear Makes Dinner

Papa Bear made dinner.

First, Papa cooked 9 carrots.
But he ate 3 of them.

Then, Papa cooked 10 green beans.
But Baby Bear ate 5 of them.

Next, Papa cooked 5 meatballs.
But he burned 3 of them.

Then, Papa baked 7 potatoes.
But 2 fell on the floor.

Finally, Papa threw everything in a big pot.
Papa said, "Let's have soup instead!"

Adding Alligators and Other Easy-to-Read Math Stories Scholastic Professional Books

Name _____ Date _____

Papa Bear Makes Dinner

Answer the questions about the story.
Write a number sentence to show each answer.
The first one has been done for you.

(1) How many carrots did Papa put in the soup?

9 − 3 = 6   6 carrots

(2) How many green beans were put in the soup?

_____ _____

(3) How many meatballs were left to put in the soup?

_____ _____

(4) How many potatoes were left to put in the soup?

_____ _____

BONUS:

How many more carrots than meatballs were put in the soup?

_____ _____

Name _____ Date _____

 Bug Crossing

The bugs needed help crossing the street.
First, Ben helped
10 ants,
10 fleas,
10 beetles,
and 10 ladybugs.

Then came
10 more ants,
10 more fleas,
10 stinkbugs,
10 crickets,
10 walking sticks,
and 10 grasshoppers.

Ben counted all the bugs that crossed the street.
But he just couldn't count all their feet!

Adding Alligators and Other Easy-to-Read Math Stories Scholastic Professional Books

Skills: Groups of 10, Addition

Name ____________________ Date ____________

Bug Crossing

On page 32, circle each group of 10.
Then answer the questions about the story.

1. How many bugs crossed the street in the first group?

   ____

2. How many bugs crossed the street in the second group?

   ____

3. How many more bugs are in the second group than in the first group? ____________

4. How many bugs crossed the street in all?

   ____

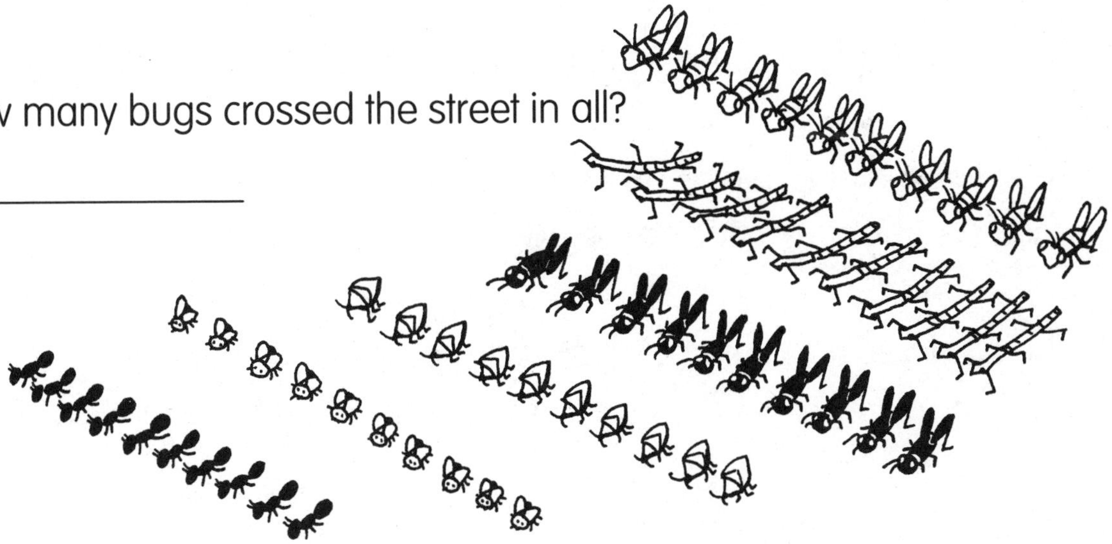

Name _____   Date _____

The 100th Day!

It was the 100th day of school.
José's class was having a party.
They didn't have time
to sing 100 songs.
They didn't have time
to play 100 games.
But they did have time
to bake and eat 100 cookies!

**Cut out the strips of cookies on page 35.
Use the cookies to solve the problems below.**

1 The students need pans to bake 100 cookies.
Each pan holds 10 cookies. How many pans do they need? _____

2 The students find bigger pans to bake 100 cookies.
Each pan holds 50 cookies. How many pans do they need? _____

3 The students have already baked 80 cookies.
How many more cookies do they need to bake to make 100? _____

4 The students have already baked 90 cookies.
How many more cookies do they need to bake to make 100? _____

Adding Alligators and Other Easy-to-Read Math Stories   Scholastic Professional Books

Name _____ Date _____

The 100th Day!

Cut out the strips of cookies.

Use the cookies to solve the problems on page 34.

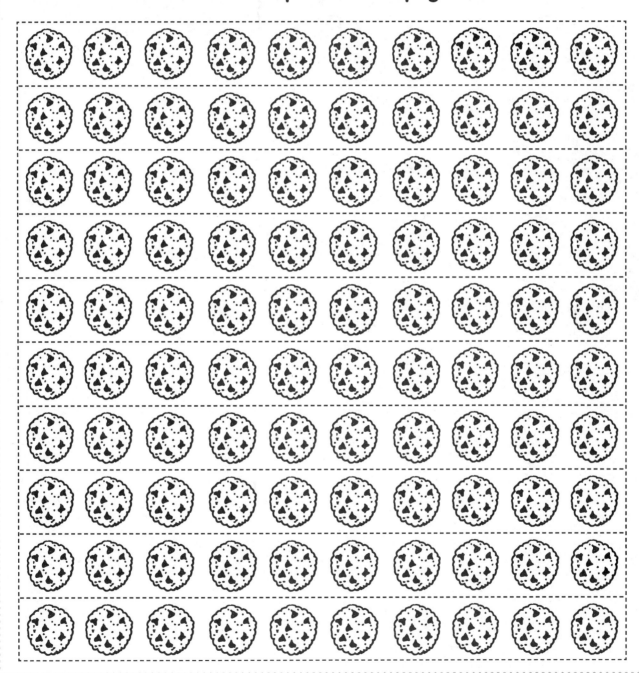

Name _____ Date _____

Going to Grandma's Farm

At 5:00 A.M. we get in the car.
We drive in the car really far.

At 7:00 A.M. we fly in a plane.
At 10:30 A.M. we take a train.

At 11:00 A.M. we get to the barn.
We get to the barn on Grandma's farm.

Once we're there,
to get somewhere
we ride her horses everywhere!

Adding Alligators and Other Easy-to-Read Math Stories   Scholastic Professional Books

Name _____ Date _____

Going to Grandma's Farm

Answer the questions about the story.

(1) The trip started at 5:00 A.M.
Draw hands on the clock to show this time.

(2) Show the time they flew in the plane.

(3) Show the time they took a train.

(4) Show the time they got to the barn.

Name _____ Date _____

Every Day Is a Special Day

Every day is a special day.

Which day do you think is my favorite day?

On Sunday I visit my Grandpa Dan.

On Monday it's library day at school.

On Tuesday I play after school with Terry.

On Wednesday school always ends early.

On Thursday we have math lab.

On Friday I take skating lessons.

On Saturday I play and play

and play all day!

Adding Alligators and Other Easy-to-Read Math Stories Scholastic Professional Books

Name _____ Date _____

Every Day Is a Special Day

Use the calendar to answer the questions.

1 Which day do you think is the child's favorite day? _____

2 Which day is the first school day of the week? _____

3 How many days are there during the weekend? _____

4 How many days are there in between Monday and Friday? _____

5 How many days are there in 1 week? _____

6 How many days are there in 2 weeks? _____

7 If Sunday is the first day of the week,
what day of the week is Wednesday?
Wednesday is the _____ day

Name _____ Date _____

There Was an Old Woman

There was an old woman
who lived in a shoe.
She had so many lizards,
she didn't know what to do.
She fed them all insects
without any bread.
Then she measured each one
from its tail to its head.

Follow the directions below.

1   Cut out the ruler on page 41.

2   Use the ruler to measure each lizard from its nose to the tip of its tail.

3   Below each lizard, write its length in inches.

4   Cut out the lizard boxes.

5   Put the lizards in order from shortest to longest.

6   Glue the lizards in order onto a sheet of paper.

Adding Alligators and Other Easy-to-Read Math Stories   Scholastic Professional Books

Name _____ Date _____

There Was an Old Woman

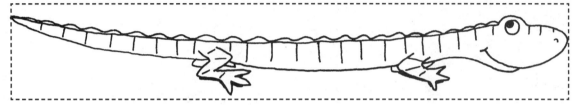

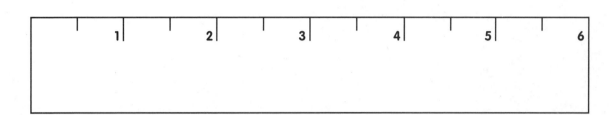

(1) _____ inches

(2) _____ inches

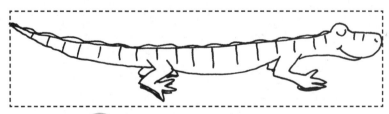

(3) _____ inches

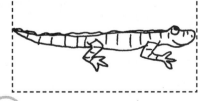

(4) _____ inches

Jenna's Missing Sock

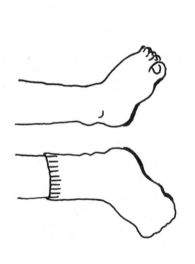

Jenna's room is so messy,
she can't find her sock.

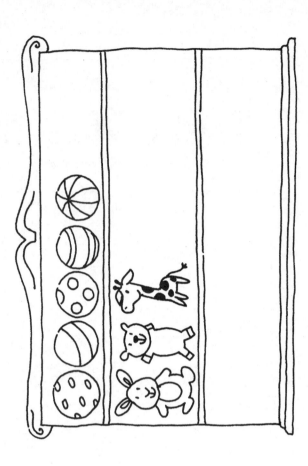

Next, Jenna puts away her stuffed animals.

First, Jenna puts away her balls.

6

What's that under the bed?

8

Do you see the graph that Jenna made?

5

Last, Jenna puts away her cars.

7

Max has Jenna's sock!

Name _____ Date _____

Jenna's Missing Sock

Use the graph to answer the questions.

1 How many balls are there? _____

2 How many stuffed animals are there? _____

3 How many cars are there? _____

4 Are there more animals or cars? _____

How many more? _____

5 Are there more animals or balls? _____

How many more? _____

6 Are there more cars or balls? _____

How many more? _____

Adding Alligators and Other Easy-to-Read Math Stories   Scholastic Professional Books

Name _____ Date _____

The Yo-Yo

Joe saw a yo-yo in the store.

It cost 45¢.

He liked it, but he didn't have any money.

Then Joe found some money.

He found a quarter in his jeans' pocket.

He found a dime in his backpack.

He found a nickel in his shoe.

He found 7 pennies in his other pocket.

Can you help Joe count his money?

Answer the questions about the story.

1 How much money did Joe find in all? _____

2 Can he buy the yo-yo? _____

3 If Joe buys the yo-yo, will he have any money left over? _____
How much? _____

4 How many more cents would Joe need to make 50¢? _____

Name _____ Date _____

 # Sam Goes Shopping

Sam went shopping.
He bought 2 pipe cleaners,
2 googly eyes,
2 felt circles,
2 felt triangles,
and a craft stick.

Sam brought everything home.
He bent the pipe cleaners.
Then he pasted everything onto a paper plate.
What did Sam make?
He made a mouse puppet for the class puppet show!

Adding Alligators and Other Easy-to-Read Math Stories Scholastic Professional Books

Skills: Money, Shapes, Doubles

Name _____ Date _____

Sam Goes Shopping

Use the prices in the picture to answer the questions.

1 How much did the 2 googly eyes cost in all? _____

2 How much did the 2 felt circles cost in all? _____

3 How much did the 2 pipe cleaners cost in all? _____

4 How much did the 2 felt triangles cost in all? _____

Name _____ Date _____

Rosy's Robot

Rosy built a robot.

It had a square head and nose.

Its body, legs, and arms were rectangles.

Its feet and mouth were circles.

Its eyes were triangles.

It had 3 fingers on each hand.

They were diamonds.

Best of all, the robot cleaned

Rosy's room every day!

Adding Alligators and Other Easy-to-Read Math Stories Scholastic Professional Books

Name _____ Date _____

Rosy's Robot

Read the story again.
Then follow the directions below.

(1) Draw the robot's head and nose.

(2) Draw the body, legs, and arms.

(3) Draw the feet and mouth.

(4) Draw the eyes.

(5) Draw the fingers.

On a separate sheet of paper, draw your own robot.

What shapes did you use? _____

What can your robot do? _____

_____

Adding Alligators and Other Easy-to-Read Math Stories   Scholastic Professional Books

Name _____ Date _____

 # Rain Forest Symmetry

In the rain forest,
I see half of a butterfly.

I see half of a leafcutter ant.

I see half of a beetle.

I see half of a snail.

What does the other half
look like?
It looks the same!

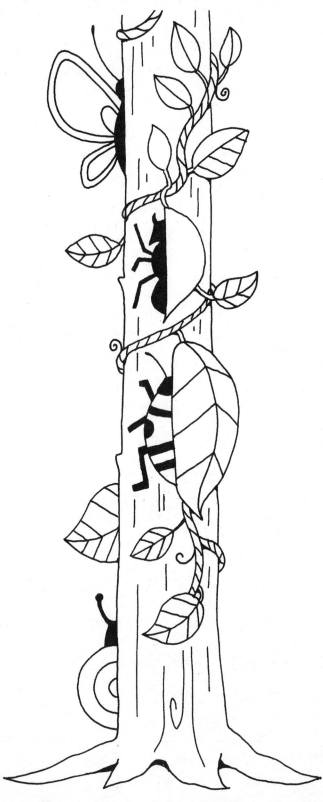

Adding Alligators and Other Easy-to-Read Math Stories Scholastic Professional Books

Name _____   Date _____

Rain Forest Symmetry

Follow the directions for each question.

1 Complete the butterfly.

2 Complete the leafcutter ant.

3 Complete the beetle.

4 Complete the snail.

── **Bonus** ──

The dashed line shows the line of symmetry on this fruit bat.

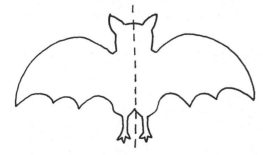

Draw the line of symmetry down the middle of this lizard.

Name _____ Date _____

 # Tom Thumb

Tom Thumb was as tall
as his father's thumb.
He had a tiny house.
He had a tiny tower to play in.
He had a tiny tent for camping.
He had a tiny baseball bat made from a toothpick.
But Tom Thumb had a great big heart
and lots of friends!

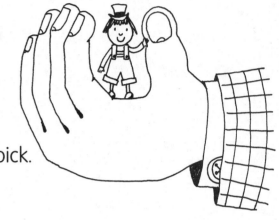

Follow the directions to make the paper models.
Then answer the questions.

1 Make Tom's house from the pattern on page 53.
Tom's house is a cube.

If you had 2 cubes, could you stack them? _____

Can you roll a cube? _____

2 Make Tom's tower from the pattern on page 54.

Tom's tower is a cylinder.

If you had 2 cylinders, could you stack them? _____

Can you roll a cylinder? _____

3 Make Tom's tent from the pattern on page 55.

Tom's tent is a pyramid.

If you had 2 pyramids, could you stack them? _____

Can you roll a pyramid? _____

Adding Alligators and Other Easy-to-Read Math Stories Scholastic Professional Books

tab

tab

tab

tab

tab

tab

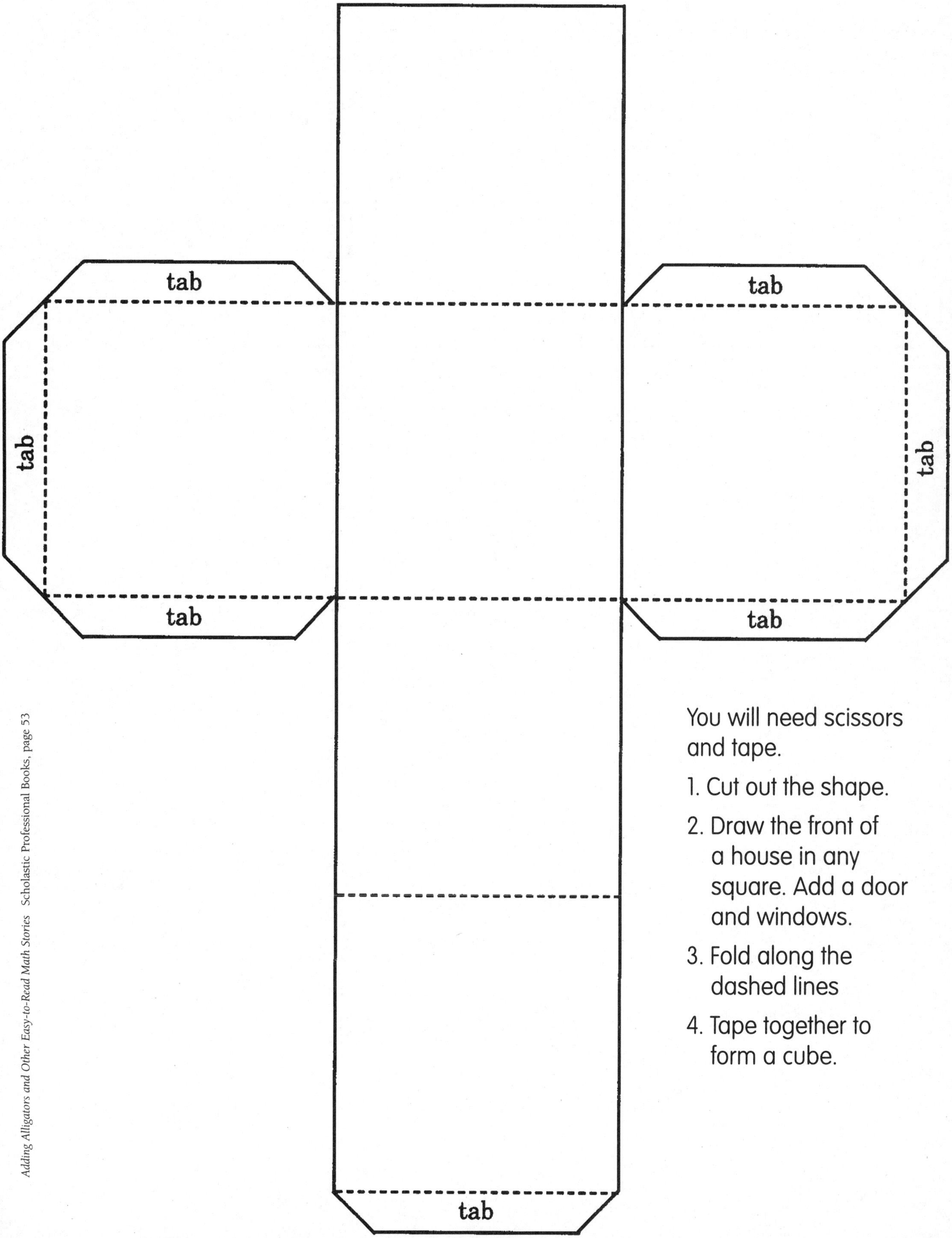

You will need scissors and tape.

1. Cut out the shape.

2. Draw the front of a house in any square. Add a door and windows.

3. Fold along the dashed lines

4. Tape together to form a cube.

Directions and Pattern for Tom's Tower

You will need scissors and tape.

1. Cut out the shape.

2. Fold along the dashed lines.

3. Roll and tape together to form a cylinder.

Directions and Pattern for Tom's Tent

You will need scissors and tape.

1. Cut out the shape.

2. Fold along the dashed lines.

3. Tape together to form a pyramid.

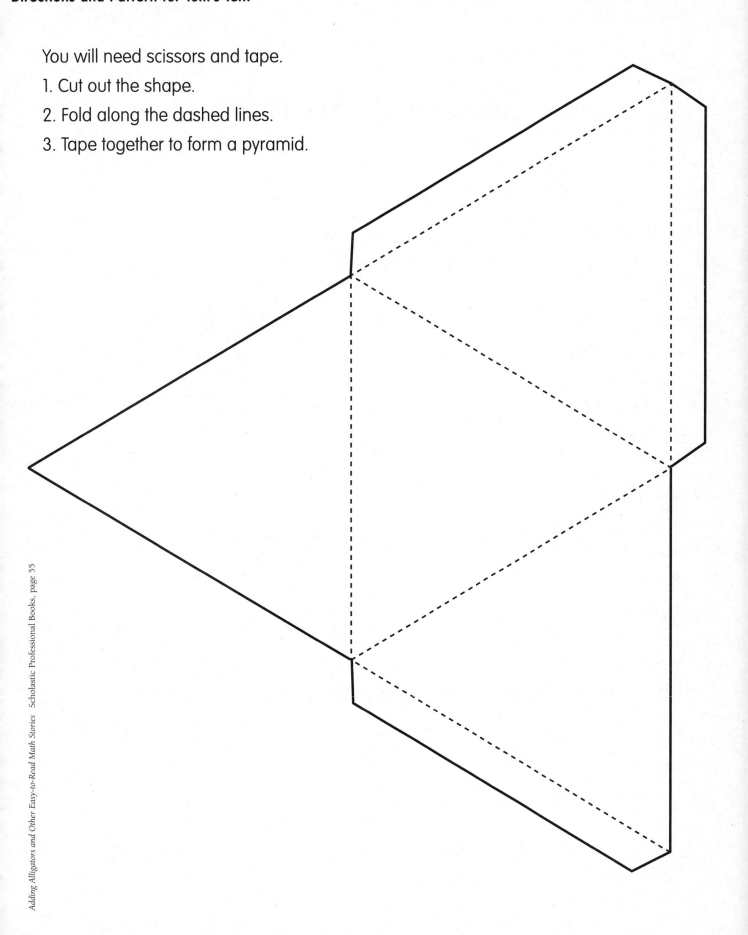

Name _____ Date _____

Sharing Snacks

It's time for snack.
It's time to share.
Sharing snacks
is fair and square!

Half for Pam
and half for Sam.

Half for Rover
and half for Grover.

Half for Joe
and half for Mo.

Half for Lee
and half for me!

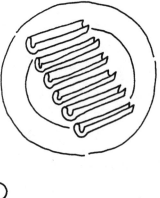
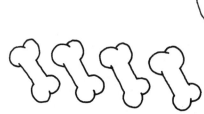

Follow the directions to color the pictures above.

1 Color ¹/₂ of the cookie.

2 Color ¹/₂ of the celery sticks.

3 Color ¹/₂ of the dog bones.

4 Color ¹/₂ of the apple slices.

Adding Alligators and Other Easy-to-Read Math Stories Scholastic Professional Books

Name _____ Date _____

Little Miss Muffet

Little Miss Muffet
sat on a tuffet
eating her toast and eggs.
Along came 2 ants
who walked on her hands.
So, she counted
the ants' tiny legs.

Use the pictures below to help you answer the questions.

1 How many legs are there on 1 ant? _____

2 How many legs are there on 2 ants? _____

3 How many legs are there on 1 ladybug? _____

4 How many legs are there on 4 ladybugs? _____

5 How many legs are there on 1 spider? _____

6 How many legs are there on 2 spiders? _____

Adding Alligators and Other Easy-to-Read Math Stories   Scholastic Professional Books

Name _____ Date _____

 # Going on a Field Trip!

The summer school class was going to the zoo.

The 12 children lined up on the sidewalk.

"How will we get there?" asked Nick.

"I don't see any cars," said Juan.

"Here come 2 cars!" said Sara.

"We won't all fit," said Nick.

Then 1 more car drove up.

There were 3 cars and 12 children.

There was enough room for everyone.

Off they went to the zoo!

Name _____ Date _____

Going on a Field Trip!

Cut out the cars and children on page 60.
Use them to help you answer the following questions.
Note: Each car fits 4 children.

(1) Suppose there were 12 children.
How many cars would they need? _____

(2) Suppose there were 16 children.
How many cars would they need? _____

(3) Suppose there were 8 children.
How many cars would they need? _____

Name _____ Date _____

Going on a Field Trip!

Adding Alligators and Other Easy-to-Read Math Stories Scholastic Professional Books

Answer Key

Sorting Circus Hats, pages 8–9
1. 3 top hats
2. 4 baseball caps
3. 5 big hats
4. 4 small hats
5. 5 gray hats
6. 4 white hats

The Farm's Asleep: A Play, pages 10–11
1. 4 cows
2. 6 sheep
3. 2 horses
4. 7 pigs
5. There are more pigs. 7 pigs > 4 cows
6. There are more sheep. 2 horses < 6 sheep
7. There are more pigs. 7 pigs > 6 sheep

The Baseball Team, pages 12–13
1. 8 seconds
2. 20 seconds
3. 12 seconds
4. 40 seconds

Pairs of Penguins, pages 14–15
1. Yes. 6 is even.
2. No. 5 is odd.
3. No. 7 is odd.
4. Yes. 8 is even.

The Animal Parade, pages 16–17
1. dog, dog, cat, cat
2. cat, dog, toad,cat, dog, toad
3. dog, cat, cat, cat, cat
4. Answers will vary.

Patterns All Around, pages 18–20

Frogs on a Log, page 21
1. The <u>fourth</u> frog has bumps on its back.
2. The <u>second</u> frog has brown dots.
3. The <u>fifth</u> frog is dark green.
4. It was the <u>sixth</u> frog to sit on the log.

Adding Alligators, pages 22–23
1. Annie used 7 blocks in all.
2. Alex ate 8 nuts in all.
3. There are 8 bears in all on Amy's mat.
BONUS: Adam has 9 counting alligators in all.

Pet Store, page 24
1. 6 + 3 = 9; 9 animals
2. 4 + 2 = 6; 6 animals
3. 6 + 5 = 11; 11 animals
4. 2 + 3 = 5; 5 animals
5. 4 + 4 = 8; 8 crabs

The Three Wishes, pages 25–27
1. 3 + 3 = 6
2. 4 + 4 = 8
3. 5 + 5 = 10
BONUS: Answers will vary.

Nina's Birthday, pages 28–29
1. 3 flies + 7 beetles = 10 bugs
2. 2 acorns + 8 walnuts = 10 nuts
3. 4 big bones + 6 small bones = 10 bones
4. 5 small worms + 5 big worms = 10 worms

Papa Bear Makes Dinner, pages 30–31
1. 9 – 3 = 6; 6 carrots
2. 10 – 5 = 5; 5 green beans
3. 5 – 3 = 2; 2 meatballs
4. 7 – 2 = 5; 5 potatoes
BONUS: 6 – 2 = 4; 4 more carrots

Bug Crossing, pages 32–33

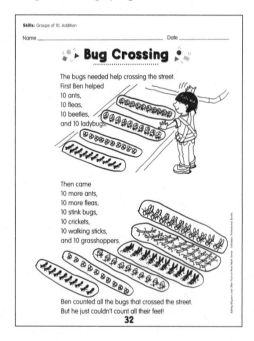

1. 40 bugs
2. 60 bugs
3. 20 bugs
4. 100 bugs

The 100th Day!, pages 34–35
1. 10 pans
2. 2 pans
3. 20 cookies
4. 10 cookies

Going to Grandma's Farm, pages 36–37

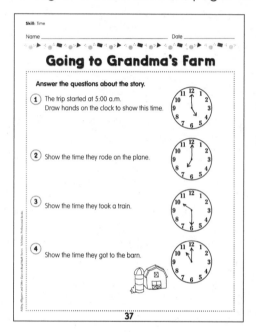

Every Day Is a Special Day, pages 38–39
1. Answers will vary.
2. Monday
3. 2 days
4. 3 days
5. 7 days
6. 14 days
7. fourth

There Was an Old Woman, pages 40–41
1. 6 inches
2. 3 inches
3. 4 inches
4. 2 inches

Jenna's Missing Sock, pages 42–44
1. There are 5 balls.
2. There are 3 stuffed animals.
3. There are 6 cars.

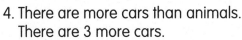

4. There are more cars than animals.
   There are 3 more cars.
5. There are more balls than animals.
   There are 2 more balls.
6. There are more cars than balls.
   There is 1 more car.

The Yo-Yo, page 45
1. Joe found 47¢.
2. Yes, Joe can buy the yo-yo.
3. Yes. He'll have 2¢ left over.
4. He would need 3¢.

Sam Goes Shopping, pages 46–47
1. The 2 eyes cost 16¢.
2. The 2 felt circles cost 18¢.
3. The 2 pipe cleaners cost 10¢.
4. The 2 felt triangles cost 12¢.

Rosy's Robot, pages 48–49
Answers will vary for the
last section.

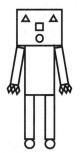

Rain Forest Symmetry, pages 50–51

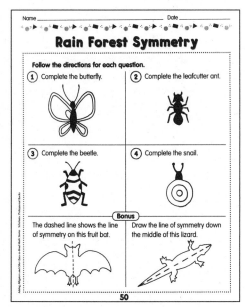

Tom Thumb, pages 52–55
1. Yes, I could stack 2 cubes.
   No, I can't roll a cube.
2. Yes, I could stack 2 cylinders.
   Yes, I can roll a cylinder.
3. No, I couldn't stack 2 pyramids.
   No, I can't roll a pyramid.

Sharing Snacks, page 56

Little Miss Muffet, page 57
1. 6 legs
2. 12 legs
3. 6 legs
4. 24 legs
5. 8 legs
6. 16 legs

Going on a Field Trip!, pages 58–60
1. 3 cars
2. 4 cars
3. 2 cars

Notes